Praise for *We Find Each Other in the Darkness*

"Richard Boada's *We Find Each Other in the Darkness* details a fractured, fragile world, a Mississippi landscape of relentless heat and morning dew, of cigarettes and distant train whistles, a world where we're aloof from both city streets and country homes. In short, a world peopled by characters from Lucinda Williams's songs: alternately tender and destructive, cruel and gracious, dazzled and disappointed by the natural world, stunned by beauty and maddened by love. Yet even as they're beaten and betrayed, as language fails them and church fails to save them—pews moved to the Amtrak station, as they chase vanishing trains—they cling to hope. If love-making only reveals a mutual loneliness, these tempo-rary communions nonetheless stir the heart to greater depths: we can't fully love or understand one another, but we can at least stand guard over one another as we live our lives."

—Paul Griner, author of *Second Life*

W0082363

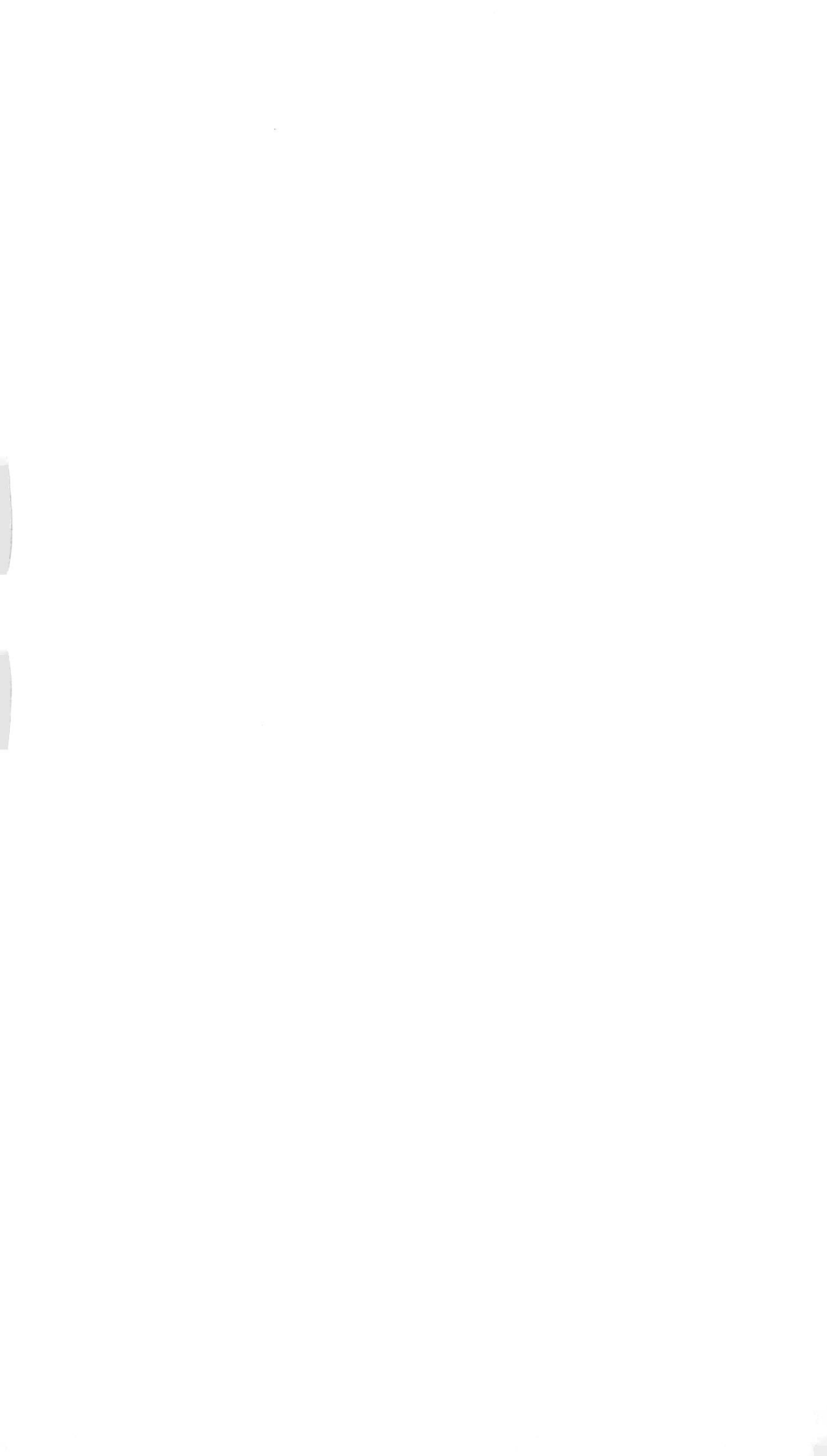

We Find Each Other in the Darkness

Texas Review Press, *publisher*
Huntsville, Texas
texasreviewpress.org

Printed in the United States of America

Library of Congress Cataloging in Publication Data
is on file at the Library of Congress, Washington, DC

Cover photo courtesy Rip Card / Flickr
Author photo courtesy Jeanne Luckett

POEMS

We Find Each Other in the Darkness

RICHARD BOADA

Texas Review Press | Huntsville, Texas

The TRP Chapbook Series

J. Bruce Fuller, *Series Editor*

The TRP Chapbook Series seeks to highlight work by either emerging authors who have not yet released their first full-length book, or established authors working on shorter projects.

Books in the series:

Richard Boada, *We Find Each Other in the Darkness*
Jose Hernandez Diaz, *The Fire Eater*
Kara Krewer, *Born-Again Anything*
Jabar Jabar, *Whatever Happened to Black Boys?*

Table of Contents

For my family

"For it is important that awake people be awake,
or a breaking line may discourage them back to sleep;
the signals we give—yes or no, or maybe—
should be clear: the darkness around us is deep."

—William Stafford

PART I

Fighting Season

If nothing gold and you can stay,
I thought I knew from the wide

stretch of navy-black sky and sawgrass
so high and wild that we'd marry and guard
our youth, again. I'd be your

husband-sentinel, crouching in front
of heavy steel trailer axles, cleaning glass,

firing coal to blasphemous heat,
and blasting away shoulders
of meat like a matador with spears.

There's a riot on the radio, they're not
the only ones with guns, blood-slick sauce

on my apron, and you, a fingerprint on my mind
like a crinkling paperback squaring against my nostalgia,
a fist in a glove ready to pop and pummel. I want

to be the lasting bloom,
the bombardier that holds back the lever.

F. Jones Corner

—Jackson, MS

I.

Snips cuticles
of his wide thumb nails
with teeth. Picks guitar
strings in quick copper
fits like leaves lift up
in wind, like trout fins
silver water.

Jackson Triptych

I. *Mississippi Zephyr*

A stag bolts into stillness.
His legs humming in the memory

of flight; antler points long
enough to reach stratospheres.

Furious rain tongues his coat.
He snorts and sloshes velocity.

How did this creature arrive
in this city—marching on Yazoo Clay

like Sherman—brown hoofs
slugging mud? I have been waiting

all along for him to prick at
my garden like a ghost

who ravages the daisies.
A city deer, now. His bewilderment

metastasizing in growing fits
like a choking man gasping for breath.

I lean against the porch rail
of my duplex to regain my strength

from the sickness of his estrangement.
Rain mellows into soft flame-like licks,

flat clouds look waterless.
There's a zephyr closing in

on the city. We hear its cringing
engine fans. My ghost has come home.

II.   *Midtown*

Houses vacant for years;
thrallings among bullet casings
and empty beer tins.
Debris electrifies us in the foundries
and print-shops. Gutted homes
blood stained and ready. On Sunday,
our neighbors bring meals—
children pull on the flapping
skirts of mothers. Palm leaf
clouds become rib cages
against a full winter moon,
its gold—translucently humid.
Angel Trumpets seduce us to twist.
If there was ever a canvas big enough
to please resentment, it bows
tonight as a white dwarf.
Skylights dazzle our skin
and I yawn like the big leaf
just about to curl from frost.

III.   *Farish Street Exit*

I'm disembarking the New Orleans
to Jackson Amtrak. A baby boy
on mother's lap who tugs
her scooping neckline bounces up
and down and she spoons
mouthfuls of Gerber's thunderously
into his soft pink mouth.
Pews in the station for us to wait.
A balding man with a younger man—
new lovers in a time of crisis.

Sky, Mississippi, sky: a laughing heart,
husky winds. Our curly mouthed
accents prolong a fear of water
contamination. Our city pipes thrum
in cold weather. Once broken,
they absorb the Yazoo Clay—
sentiments of soft earth—
and our water darkens. Home, I drink it,
and my body cranks-up like a forest fire—at once
a clinching organ and shadow.

The Sky Over Jackson

Alone with the hydrangeas
purchased at the grocery store in Midtown

and unevenly planted in the clay,
my body was once like that ecosystem

alight with invertebrates, and I would
become one, a vessel of soft tissue reddened

and enlightened. I look through a sequence
of trees, black limbs mossed and dewy

for the galaxy undone. I'm bringing
my bony knots into thanksgiving for the waxing

night lolls. I don't have what it takes
to ask a meaningful question
of its circumference or grace.

Not an Age for Saving

A man directs his eyes our way
but keeps head still, transfixed
in conversation. "They're assassins.
And there go the investigators. They eat
breakfast at Walker's every Tuesday."
His dark skin signals restlessness. Goose pimples
salute hot January sun. Ribs, ship beams
under construction, rise visible through white
sleeveless cotton tee. His heavy work jeans
bunch and squint around the ankles. We enter
the cigarette shop and his organs
relax. He breathes, buys a copy of the paper. We play
the scratchoffs on the counter. The copper bell
on the door pings. He clutches
my forearm, the coin stutters on the ticket
like flat chalk on sidewalks. Gray shavings spill
on the floor. He whispers that we could smuggle
ourselves out of the country with the winnings.
It's an old habit. I remind him there's no need.
We carry American passports. We're no longer refugees.

I Can't Get Rid of this Hate

Gray Mississippi kites flock,
their banded tails whipping air.
Young frogs hunker down
in wild grass. Dragonflies skim
the pond's stillness. Red-throated
loons wade on its surface. I bury
seeds along the shaded
wiry thicket. My mouth
contorted from a pinch of snuff
wedged beside my gums. Black spit
leaks onto my beard. I yank buds
off mature stalks, shoot
at a gallery of herons with a rifle,
walk away empty.

The Other End of Lonesomeness

Limbs hang upon each
other; tentacles of winter.
I sleep beside an oak,
red boughs bend.
A leaf sails with its veins
exposed, it fondles
the earth's charcoal
surface with each tumble.
Homespun moonshine
settles. Yazoo hills
smell of bourbon mash
and marijuana. Ice will
collect in the shadows
where the cold adheres.

Confession of Solitude

He hunkers into breakfast, sops egg
yolk with wheat toast, flats ovals

of milk on the plastic table
with the back of his spoon. She blasts the horn

and he scuttles out of the house shoving
his pressed uniform shirt down the back

of his slacks. She drives them up
the utility truck road

and parks under the water-tower
where they fuck long enough to confess

the darkness between them is inseparable
from their mercies.

Confess There's a Wound

Sober, she pulls cigarette smoke dry hard
with wrinkled lips holding. Longer violent
ember races to the filter, snapping
thin paper reeling. Its crisp tobacco
disappears into her body, a way,

scattered through her nostrils against my taut
cedar-like neck. Craned, shaved smooth to my ears
because a jaw's shape determines how well
you confess something sacred, how you hold your eyes
to other eyes in dark rooms. She's lived in Mississippi

too long, with weightless air, and we dismiss
each other's habits. A match filliped spit
light, our lips navigating, she holds the fire.

PART II

F. Jones Corner

—Jackson, MS

II.

The flesh, it turns
and slimes. Pinched
heels bleed through
black wool. He two-steps
facing the music, toes pointed
down, trying to get
rid of his hate.

Us in a Mirror

It's done. Our faces fire
in expressionless orange.
Her hard violent lips pull
ember to the filter. Snapping
thin paper reels. Crisp tobacco
burns, departs into her body, rifles
through her nostrils against my jaw.
I flick the match into the toilet,
it hisses in water. Ash falls
on tile. Our torsos swallowed
by the room's dismissive gray.
Rosined muscles, taut,
she prepares to breathe for one.

What Can I Tell You That You Don't Already Know?

You flattened the bedspread on your side
with palms swift and no longer delicate,

militantly tucked a corner, and I pretended to sleep, curled
in the terror of who I'd become. My waking

wouldn't prevent the separation. Dresser drawers
cringed and squealed, no folding for the packing

suitcases tossed down the hallway like Olympic hammers.
Your body twirled for momentum and the heft.

There was the house and the longleaf pines wet
from fresh sleet-pack so thin and nearly invisible.

The sedan gunned in reverse, you vanished and I
absorbed the improbable morning darkness.

Water's Price

Our cisterns emptied months ago
in police raids. Our stolen water
thrown to the ground, let go. At night,
when in rains, neighbors set out plastic
bails on their porches, most with rope
handles, underneath the dripping.
They arrange cups and bowls on flat roofs.
I pinch the house candlelights off,
move indoor containers out, reconnect
drain pipes from the sewer. We want
fast, heavy rains to fill. No one tells
where water went.

Hands-Free Flushing

We're amnesiacs taking
possession of consonants.
We halve white

tablets, scatter them
on gilded shaving
tray, swallow Bob Dylan

—the topical. His fingers
sire more than dissent.
We consume

too much saltwater. Our tongues
melt. They're stinted,
vowels bolted up in stalls.

Electric Hunger

A nice looking man, say in his forties,
blue triggering eyes, thin boxy hair, taller
than me, asks for the time, and I stop walking,

turn left over shoulder, bend eyes for the watch
on my wrist and he yells a Hail Mary, hates in
his prayer. Purpled veins

peak and blow up on his croaking cheeks.
Spits down through teeth, gums a dark marsh.
Hates more in prayer. He follows me with a throat

that concedes to the voices around us. Feeding electric
hunger, I want fists to charge prayer back into his mouth.

Ripening Morning

I pull open thin cotton
curtains; they squint
from sunlight, gauze wrap
dust beads. I hook metal
buttons on corduroy overalls,
lace-up boots. Dew webs
on the tired laundry lines
heavy with quilts. A train
roughs the distance.

She chain-smokes
in her kitchen. Boils
water, rinses berries
in a cauldron. Steeps
tea. She lifts
the mattress out
of the couch, unfolds
its curves. Smoothens
sheets. Cigarette ash
falls on carpet.

I knock on her back door;
she lets me in and I lap
up the smoke
off her chest,
taste unbroken habit
in her mouth.

PART III

F. Jones Corner

—Jackson, MS

III.

"There was this girl in Italy and who can remember
the town. Men crowded to light her cigarette," says the
    bartender
to no one in particular, and I'm a live one with the heat of
    the whisky.

Another Mercy

Unfinished *Pietà*. Hands reach
for would-be folds

in the Virgin's shroud.
So far from definition,

shapes remain quadrangular.
Resigned to smooth

cankerous grains he
hammers and files

the marble cortex. He suspects
Christ's masculine tendons

would have sagged
there, on his mother's

lap. The place
where active cells

failed to synapse, failed
to reach voluntary muscles.

Guerrera

She's no longer afraid of dying. Tonight,
she'll hand customers back pocket change

and credit card slips. She'll hang her apron
in a locker, punch a time card right

on the hour and slip the night manager a smile.
She'll hop up and over the customer service counter,

snag a pint of whisky and jet out of the store. She'll chase
the Union Southern on foot along Main

until it steers away for Hammond and New Orleans.
She'll find a grassy quay on the canal. The damp

night grass will soak through her clothes. Fingers of light
from distant cars will dazzle her until she's finished.

Here We Are

I go to bed with you under the pretext that I'd read to you
first from the book I mailed you as a gift

because you would know me better if you could hear me
rather than just imagine me in your voice and making love

would become more glamor than a tilting within
    ourselves.
It turns out you don't mind that swanning intent but
    rather prefer the evil

of my voice without the recitation of poems I'd never feel
    so like myself
sitting cross-legged on your full-sized bed facing you

in the streetlight weaning through the tacked window
    drapes and here we are
the ecosystem of falsehood exactly what we endure

from being loved like that. You are there and I want you
to know one thing about the atoms navigating between us

as if I could reach into that book and tell you how things
    would turn
out, a prophecy of second marriages longed for.

Mississippi Winter Crows

I'm trying to harness the arrangement
of the cosmos and the new

republic of distant light
that will unlatch you

from this murder of Mississippi
crows drinking leadened city water

in the parking lot of the Metrocenter Mall,
a monument to infidelity and palimpsests

so fragile. I keep trying to see you
against the tundraed cement,

a gravity of cosmos belching pink
sunlight, but instead I miss your hands

and the absence of their pressure
like prints engraved forever on my bosom.

No One Belongs Here More Than You

You've been told about knife-fights
with ghosts and church bells

that would remind people to drink
water on fearlessly hot days. You knew

this town as a younger man with a new lover
and the darkness of Mississippi highways with bruins

observing the burning fields. You've been double-crossed
and now must brace yourself to drink again

the pattern of the levee, a wasting away of slicking clay,
a return that threatens to undo you all over.

Acknowledgments

"Jackson Triptych." *Urban Voices: 51 Poems from
    51 American Poets*, San Francisco, Bay Press
"Mississippi Winter Crows." *Poetry South*
"No One Belongs Here More Than You." *Poetry South*
"Fighting Season." *Town Creek Poetry*
"The Sky Over Jackson." *Town Creek Poetry*
"What Can I Tell You That You Don't Already Know?"
    Town Creek Poetry
"Mississippi Zephyr." *North American Review*
"Hands-Free Flushing." *Northridge Review*